THE WEAPONS ENCYCLOPÆDIA
TANK AIRCRAFT AFV SHIP ARTILLERY VEHICLES SECRET WEAPON

TWE-035 ENG

AUTOBLINDO AS42, S37, AS43, AS43 ARMOURED CAR & LINCE

THE WEAPONS ENCYCLOPAEDIA

EDITORIAL STAFF

Luca Cristini, Paolo Crippa.

ACADEMIC STAFF

Enrico Acerbi, Massimiliano Afiero, Aldo Antonicelli, Ruggero Calò, Luigi Carretta, Flavio Chistè, Anna Cristini, Carlo Cucut, Salvo Fagone, Enrico Finazzer, Arturo Giusti, Björn Huber, Andrea Lombardi, Aymeric Lopez, Marco Lucchetti, Gabriele Malavoglia, Luigi Manes, Giovanni Maressi, Francesco Mattesini, Daniele Notaro, Péter Mujzer, Federico Peirani, Alberto Peruffo, Maurizio Raggi, Andrea Alberto Tallillo, Antonio Tallillo, Roberto Vela, Massimo Zorza.

PUBLISHED BY

Luca Cristini Editore (Soldiershop), via Orio, 35/4 - 24050 Zanica (BG) ITALY.

DISTRIBUTION BY

Soldiershop - www.soldiershop.com, Amazon, Ingram Spark, Berliner Zinnfigurem (D), LaFeltrinelli, Mondadori, Libera Editorial (Spain), Google book (eBook), Kobo, (eBoook), Apple Book (eBook).

PUBLISHING'S NOTES

None of unpublished images or text of our book may be reproduced in any format without the expressed written permission of Luca Cristini Editore (already Soldiershop.com) when not indicate as marked with license creative commons 3.0 or 4.0. Luca Cristini Editore has made every reasonable effort to locate, contact and acknowledge rights holders and to correctly apply terms and conditions to Content. Every effort has been made to trace the copyright of all the photographs. If there are unintentional omissions, please contact the publisher in writing at: info@soldiershop.com, who will correct all subsequent editions.

LICENSES COMMONS

This book may utilize part of material marked with license creative commons 3.0 or 4.0 (CC BY 4.0), (CC BY-ND 4.0), (CC BY-SA 4.0) or (CC0 1.0). We give appropriate attribution credit and indicate if change were made in the acknowledgments field. Our WTW books series utilize only fonts licensed under the SIL Open Font License or other free use license.

CONTRIBUTORS OF THIS VOLUME & ACKNOWLEDGEMENTS

We would like to thank the main contributors to this issue: The profiles of the floats are all by the author. The colouring of the photos is by Anna Cristini. Special thanks to national and/or private institutions such as: Army General Staff, State Archives, Bundesarchiv, Nara, Library of Congress, Wikipedia, USAF, Signal magazine, War Chronicles, War Front, IWM, Australian War Museum, etc. A P.Crippa, A.Lopez, Péter Mujzer, L.Manes, C.Cucut, Tallillo archives. Model Victoria (www.modelvictoria.it) etc. for providing images or other items from their archives.

For a complete list of Soldiershop titles, or for every information please contact us on our website: www.soldiershop.com or www.cristinieditore.com. E-mail: info@soldiershop.com. Keep up to date on Facebook https://www.facebook.com/soldiershop.publishing

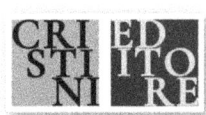

Title: **AUTOBLINDO AS42, S37, AS43, AS43 ARMOURED CAR & LINCE** Code.: **TWE-035 EN** Series by L. S. Cristini
ISBN code: 9791255892083 First edition February 2025
THE WEAPONS ENCYCLOPAEDIA (SOLDIERSHOP) is a trademark of Luca Cristini Editore

THE WEAPONS ENCYCLOPÆDIA
TANK AIRCRAFT AFV SHIP ARTILLERY VEHICLES SECRET WEAPON

AUTOBLINDO AS42, S37, AS43, AS43 ARMOURED CAR & LINCE

LUCA STEFANO CRISTINI

BOOK SERIES FOR MODELERS & COLLECTORS

CONTENTS

Introduction .... pag. 5

AS 42 "Sahariana" .... pag. 7

Fiat SPA S37 .... pag. 23

SPA VIBERTI AS 43 .... pag. 29

AS 43 "Desertica" Armoured car .... pag. 37

Autoblindo Lancia "Lince" .... pag. 43

Autoblindo operational use .... pag. 49

Camouflage and markings .... pag. 54

Production and export .... pag. 56

Bibliography .... pag. 58

▲ Beautiful photo of the AS42 armoured car taken in the middle of the Libyan desert. Interesting for the overview of the weapons on board the vehicle.

INTRODUCTION

This volume marks the third installment in a series devoted to Italian armored cars used during World War II. After dealing in the first volume with the Lancia 1Z and the FIAT 611 and the second volume devoted to the AB 40/41/42/43 armored cars, it is time to focus on remaining models that are more representative of the evolution of the Italian armored forces, starting with the **Autoblinda AS 42** and all the others that appeared between the late 1930s and the end of the war. As for *the "Sahariana,"* its importance in the desert war and in the various theaters of operation in Africa, Greece, Russia and other fronts made it a key reference point for understanding the technological and tactical evolution of Italian armored vehicles during the conflict.

Italian armored cars, particularly those developed since the early 1940s, were an integral part of the armed forces of the Kingdom of Italy during World War II. Each model represented a response to changing strategic needs, from the need for faster and more agile means of reconnaissance and mobile troop support to adaptation to the specific conditions of various theaters of operation. The AS 42, designed by Viberti first and taken over by Fiat-Ansaldo later, fits into this context as one of the most advanced and functional Italian armored cars, known for their robustness and versatility, particularly appreciated in desert environments.

Other vehicles, such as the **AS 43 Desertica** truck and the **SPA Viberti 43,** also deserve special attention, as they reflect the attempts of the Italian war industry to adapt to the conditions of desert warfare and to meet the needs of the conflict in North Africa, where Italy, an ally of Germany, was fighting against Allied forces.

The AS 42 armored cars, in particular, represent a mature phase of the Italian light armored project. With improved armor, more powerful engine, and greater armament capacity, the AS 42 was able to cope with the difficulties of the desert and support Italian operations during the long North African campaign. The variants we are going to analyze are examples of how tactical and logistical requirements could be met by increasingly specialized vehicles optimized for a given type of environment and mission.

In this volume, we will explore in detail not only the technical specifications and modifications of the different versions of the AS 42, but also its operational use in various scenarios, with a focus on the campaigns in North Africa, where these vehicles played a crucial role in the context of Afrika Korps operations and Italian forces. All other armored cars/trucks not addressed in previous volumes will also complete the volume: the **AS 37**, **SPA AS 43**, the **Viberti SPA AS 43** desert truck, and finally the **Lince**!

The **Fiat-SPA AS Autoprotetto S37** was an armored troop transport vehicle produced by the Società Piemontese Automobili (SPA) and adopted by the Royal Army during World War II. Somewhat derived from this was the AS43 or SPA-Viberti AS43 vehicle, an armored car produced by Viberti and adopted by the Army of the Italian Social Republic during World War II.

Another very interesting vehicle was the **Fiat-SPA AS43** or **SPA-Viberti AS43,** Like the AS 42, this was an armed Saharan truck employed mainly in the European theater by the armed forces of the Italian Social Republic and Nazi Germany during World War II.

We will finish by talking about the last born, the **Lince**, whose full name was: **Lancia Ansaldo Lince**; it is an armored car produced in Italy by Lancia Veicoli Industriali in collaboration with Ansaldo, during World War II, in about 263 examples. Made on the inspiration of the British Daimler Scout Car better known as the "Daimler Dingo," due to the fact that some examples were captured in Libya.

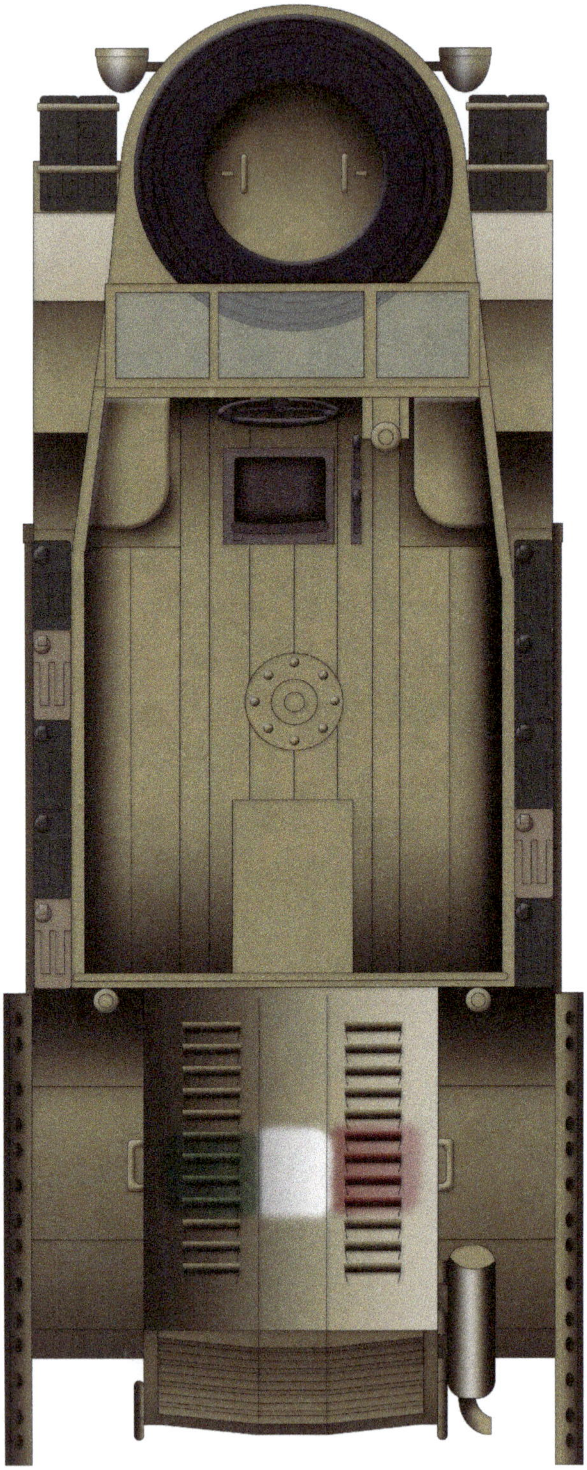

▲ AS 42 'Saharan' armoured car profile from above.

AS 42 "SAHARIANA"

THE ARMORED VEHICLE IN THE DESERT

The Autoblinda AS 42 Sahariana is undoubtedly one of the most fascinating and iconic variants of the AS 42. Designed to cope with the hardships of the North African desert during World War II, the Sahariana represented a highly adapted solution to arid and sandy environments.

This chapter examines the genesis, technical characteristics, variants and operational use of the AS 42 Saharan, analyzing how the vehicle adapted to the extreme conditions of the desert and became one of the stars of the Italian armed forces during the campaigns in Africa.

DEVELOPMENT

Historical Context and Operational Needs

In the context of World War II, the North African campaign, fought between 1940 and 1943, was characterized by its logistical, climatic and geographical difficulties. The fighting between Axis and Allied forces took place in an arid environment, with vast expanses of sand and temperatures reaching extremely high levels during the day. Motorized vehicles had to cope with difficult terrain and the need for continuous supplies, as well as having to counter enemy forces in open terrain with no natural cover.

Conventional armored cars, such as the AS 42, were effective in more diverse terrain, but they were not designed to operate in the desert, where fine sand and high temperatures could have compromised their mobility and durability. The Italian Army, recognizing the need for an armored vehicle specifically designed for desert operations, decided to develop a special version of the AS 42: the Sahariana.

Saharan Project and Development

The basis for creating the AS 42 Saharan was the same as the standard AS 42, but numerous modifications were made to improve its ability to operate in desert conditions. The first prototype of this version was built in 1941, and large-scale production began in the following months. The special feature of the design was the structural modifications, which made the vehicle more suitable for the climate and terrain of the North African desert.

One of the main changes concerned the suspension system and wheels. The AS 42 Saharan was fitted with wider and stronger wheels, designed to avoid the phenomenon of "sinking" into sandy soil. Tire pressure was reduced to ensure more even weight distribution, allowing the vehicle to traverse the quicksand without becoming trapped. Speed, which was one of the crucial aspects in the desert, was improved, as the armored cars had to be able to quickly travel long distances between supply points and battle lines.

In addition, the armor of the AS 42 Saharan was lightened in some sections to reduce overall weight and improve maneuverability, without compromising crew protection from small arms and explosive fragments. The top of the armor was also modified to reduce the accumulation of dust and sand, which could have compromised the operation of the vehicle's engines and other vital systems.

TECHNICAL FEATURES

The AS 42 Autoblinda was distinguished by a balance of protection, speed and maneuverability. Although it was not equipped with particularly thick armor, the vehicle's design aimed to offer sufficient protection against light gunfire and explosive fragments, while the wheels allowed for greater mobility than tracked tanks.

▲ AS 42 'Saharan' armoured car profile front and rear view.

AUTOBLINDO AS42 "SAHARIANA", NOTHERN AFRICA, 1940

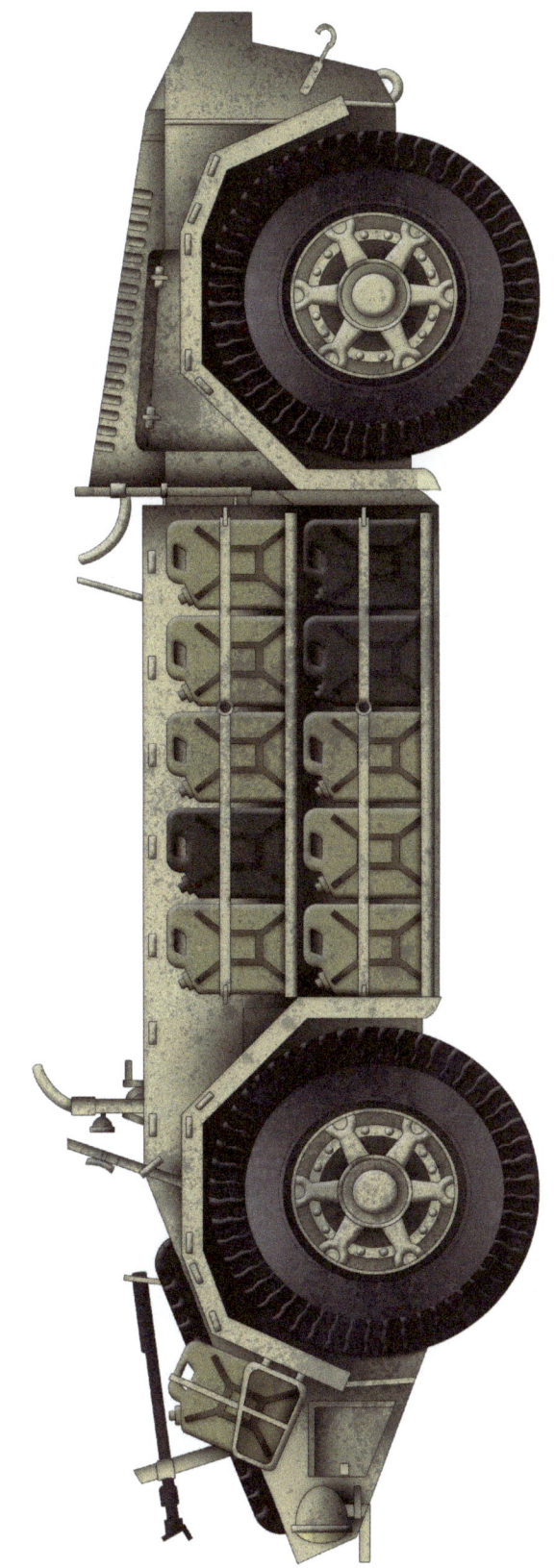

▲ Armoured Truck SPA Viberti/Fiat AS 42 Desert Saharan. Featuring a low, elegant line. Immediately recognisable thanks to the double row of petrol cans on the sides of the vehicle. It was part of the Royal Army's Saharan Regiment in Africa 1942-43.

AUTOBLINDO AS42 "SAHARIANA", NORTHERN AFRICA 1942-1943

▲▼ Two different visions of the SPA Viberti/Fiat AS 42 Saharan desert armoured car. Both coloured in the sandy yellow camouflage chosen by the Royal Army's Saharan grouping in Africa 1942-43.

A very versatile and reliable vehicle, it was designed for a good variety of functions, and consequently armed with a main weapon that could be an anti-tank gun (pictured above), the Breda 20mm heavy machine gun, which could be dismounted for ground operations, and even an anti-tank gun derived from the well-known 47/32 'Elefantino'. The vehicle, in order to withstand the intense desert heat, also had a canvas cover, as seen in the model below.

Structure and Armor

The AS 42 was built on a welded steel frame, with armor ranging from 8 to 30 millimeters thick. The front and side of the body were better protected, while the rear and top had lighter armor. This provided adequate protection against hits from machine guns and other weapons of lower caliber, but was not designed to withstand direct hits from heavier guns. The shape of the body was sloping to help deflect bullets and reduce the likelihood of direct damage, a principle that followed the architecture of the most advanced armored vehicles of the time.

Engine and Performance

The AS 42 was equipped with a Fiat SPA 18A gasoline engine, an 88-horsepower inline 8-cylinder, which allowed the vehicle to reach a top speed of about 80 km/h on the road and about 35 km/h off-road. The engine, while not particularly powerful for an armored vehicle, provided good speed due to the vehicle's relatively low weight, which hovered around 5,000 kg. Wheel drive, with all-wheel drive on both axles, enabled the AS 42 to tackle difficult terrain, such as sand and slush, without compromising performance too much.

The suspension system was coil spring, which helped to maintain some stability even on uneven terrain. This aspect was critical in operations in harsh environments, such as the desert, where rough and sandy terrain posed significant challenges to the mobility of armored vehicles.

▶ Desertica SPA-Viberti AS42 'Sahariana' truck covered by waterproof tarpaulin. Image taken inside the premises of Officine Viberti in Turin (Courtesy of Claudio Pergher via Enrico Finazzer).

▲ The crew of a SPA-Viberti AS42 'Saharan' Desert Truck is filmed during a break in the fighting. Equipped with the Breda Model 1938 medium machine gun in the front, without an upper magazine. Also interesting is the use of the windscreen to 'rest' the barrel of the anti-tank gun.

AUTOBLINDO SPA VIBERTI / FIAT AS42 "SAHARIANA", NORTHERN AFRICA, 1942-43

▲ SPA Viberti AS 42 Saharan desert armoured car armed with a Breda 20mm machine gun, and a Solothurn rifle, belonging to a 'Saharan' company of the Royal Army's Desert Regiment, Tunisia, March 1943. In the small image: a light variant of the same.

Carrying capacity and crew

The AS 42 was designed for a crew of four men: a driver, a tank leader, a gunner, and a gunner. The vehicle had a length of about 5.6 meters, a width of 2.5 meters, and a height of about 2.1 meters, providing ample space for the crew, albeit in a confined environment. The compact size was ideal for ensuring maneuverability and versatility in the field, but limited the loading capacity for ammunition and supplies.

The interior of the AS 42 was designed to protect the crew against gunfire and shrapnel, with ergonomic seats and equipment to enable rapid combat operations. Visibility for the driver and other crew members was limited compared to other vehicles, but offset by the rotating turret that provided a good field of view for the commander and gunner.

Wheels and Maneuverability

Another distinctive aspect of the AS 42 was the use of wheels instead of traditional

▶ Front and rear view of a SPA-Viberti AS42 'Saharan' desert truck with windscreen covered by a waterproof tarpaulin. The vehicle is ready for delivery, obviously unarmed and without a tripod for the machine gun. The number plates, like the armament, were also added after delivery to the army. The vehicle is equipped with Pirelli 'Raiflex' tyres. (Courtesy of Claudio Pergher via Enrico Finazzer).

▲ AS 42 Saharan armed with a 20 mm Solothurn anti-tank gun. Since the beginning of the war, the Italians have had specialised units for the control of the interior desert, the Saharan Auto-Avio Companies. At first on AS37 lorries and then on 'Saharans', both efficient and well-armed vehicles, they fought in the defence of the oases and against Anglo-French penetration.

AUTOBLINDO SPA VIBERTI /FIAT AS42 "SAHARIANA II" METRPOLITANA, ITALY, SEPTEMBER 1943

▲ Armoured car Camionetta SPA Viberti/Fiat AS 42 Sahariana II 'Metropolitana' armed with Cannoncino 47/32, belonging to the motorised assault battalion, Rome, September 1943.

belts. This allowed the vehicle to move quickly on the road and cover great distances without the need for heavy maintenance. The wheels were large in size, equipped with strong tires that could cope with the difficult desert terrain without compromising speed too much. In addition, the coil spring suspension conferred good shock-absorbing ability even when maneuvering over rough terrain.

Deployment and Adaptability
Although the AS 42's technical characteristics did not make it suitable for combat against heavy tanks, they made it extremely versatile as a reconnaissance and support armored car in harsh environments. The balance between protection and speed made it ideal for operations in rough terrain and harsh environmental conditions, such as those of the North African desert, where sandy terrain and high temperatures tested the capabilities of many other vehicles.

ARMAMENT

The armament of the Autoblinda AS 42 varied depending on the version and the specific needs of the theater of operations. Italian armored cars were designed for versatile use, with different armament options that allowed them to adapt to both reconnaissance and direct troop support missions. Listed below are the main weapons that could be mounted on the AS 42 and its variants as needed.

▲ A SPA-Viberti AS42 'Metropolitana' truck of the Motorised Assault Battalion armed with a Model 1935 47/32 gun and a Model 1937 Breda Medium Machine Gun. The picture was taken in Rome in the convulsive days following the armistice (N. Arena).

▲ A nice picture, again set in the North African theatre, showing an AS42 truck equipped with the 47/32 anti-tank gun of the same type, used in the profile on the opposite page. In this case, however, it is not the Metropolitan version, which, as is well known, gave up the canister pockets, either both or only one, in place of capable spaces for loading the gun shells with which the vehicle was equipped.

The Breda Mod. 37 represented one of the main machine guns used on the vehicle. It was a medium machine gun, capable of using 24-round magazines. The Breda Mod. 37 was a reliable and relatively light weapon capable of providing good supporting fire against enemy infantry forces and light vehicles.

For combat against enemy armored vehicles or more robust targets, the AS 42 could be equipped with the **Solothurn S-18/1000**, a 20-mm anti-tank gun. This anti-tank rifle used 10-round magazines and proved particularly useful against light armored vehicles, although its effectiveness was limited against heavier vehicles or tanks. The use of this armament reflected the need for Italian forces to equip themselves with weapons capable of dealing with early threats from enemy armored vehicles.

Another armament employed was the **Breda 20/65 Mod. 1935**, a 20 mm anti-aircraft machine gun. This type of weapon, also used in a mobile version, was capable of fighting both air and ground targets, such as enemy aircraft or light armored vehicles. The magazines of the Breda 20/65 held 12 rounds and were used in situations where protection from air attack and the ability to hit fast targets were priorities.

As for the main armament, the AS 42 could be equipped with the 47/32 **Mod 35 cannon**, a 47 mm anti-tank gun. This cannon was capable of dealing with light and medium armored vehicles, although its effectiveness against heavier tanks was limited. The 47/32 gun was one of the most common choices for Italian armored cars, especially in versions intended to support operations in North Africa, where armored forces were an increasing danger.

In addition to the standard armament, as reported by many photos and newsreels of the time, non-standard or additional armaments were also mounted in several AS 42s. These included **Breda Mod. 38** and **Breda Mod. 30** machine guns, light weapons that were readily available and capable of being mounted on homemade mounts. These machine guns, while not original to the AS 42, were adapted to the needs of the departments in the field and used in scenarios where additional firepower could make a difference.

In addition, some armored cars were modified to mount weapons captured during operations. Among the most common were **British Vickers K** machine guns, in both single and double barrel versions. These armaments had been captured during clashes with British forces in the desert, and were later adapted and mounted on Italian armored cars. The use of captured armament, unfortunately not always perfectly integrated with the vehicle, became a common practice, especially when resources and domestically produced ammunition were scarce.

▲ Left: detail view of the interior of the AS42 'Sahariana' from above, highlighting the comfortable space used by the vehicle's crew. Right: a pair of SPA-Viberti AS42 'Sahariana' Desert Trucks engaged in the crossing of a small ford in the North African theatre of operations, an environment for which this vehicle was particularly made.

DATA SHEET AS 42 "Sahariana"	
Dimensions	5.6 length x 2.26 width x 1.80 height (in m)
Weight	4,5 t
Crew	5
Entering and leaving service	December 1942 - 1954
Fuel capacity	145 l in the tank + 400 l in the canisters
Engine	SPA Abm 1 in-line 6-cylinder, petrol-driven, water-cooled
Maximum speed	90 km/h on road, 37km/h off road
Autonomy	535 km on the road, 1200 km with tanks, 17 hours off-road
Power	110 CV
Armament	1 x 13.2 mm or 20 mm machine gun or a 20 mm anti-tank gun or a 47 mm gun
Secondary armament	1 or 2 8 mm machine guns
Traction	4-wheel drive and steering
Production	About 140 Saharan I and another 50 Saharan II Metropolitana
Users	Royal Army, German Army, National Republican Army Italy, Italian State Police.

▲ An AS 42 II "Metropolitan" truck: soldiers of the 2.Fsch.Jg.Division of the German army on the eastern front, winter 1943.

AUTOBLINDO SPA VIBERTI /FIAT AS42 "SAHARIANA II" METRPOLITANA, UKRAINE, URSS 1943

▲ SPA Viberti/Fiat AS 42 Saharan II "Metropolitan" armoured car armed with 47/32 cannon, used on the Eastern Front in the Ukraine, USSR, in the winter of 1943.

AUTOBLINDO SPA VIBERTI /FIAT AS42 "SAHARIANA II" METRPOLITANA, ITALY 1943-1954

▲ Armoured car Camionetta SPA Viberti/Fiat AS 42 Sahariana II 'Metropolitana' armed with 20mm Breda machine gun, belonging to the national police force and painted in the characteristic amaranth red colour. Also in use after the war until 1954.

▲ Another picture of the AS 42 II "Metropolitan" truck carrying soldiers of the 2.Fsch.Jg.Division of the German Army on the Eastern Front, winter 1943.
▼ Lieutenant Carlo Pettini's AS42 'Metropolitana' truck from the 'Cheren' Column was hit by a US M3 Stuart in Via Nazionale on 4 June 1944. None of the six PAI officers on board survived. A crowd of curious civilians surrounds the vehicle to try to understand what happened.

THE OTHER VERSION OF AS 42: LA METROPOLITANA

The Autoblinda AS 42, although the flagship version among Italian light armored vehicles of World War II, did not remain a static configuration. As operations and wartime needs continued, several similar variants of the vehicle were developed, each adapted to specific tactical and environmental requirements. Of these, the **SPA Viberti 43**, **AS 43 Desert**, and **Lince** versions represented some of the most important models, each with unique characteristics that determined its operational use and success in different combat conditions. While directly from the AS42 derived mainly a version called theMetropolitanaor AS 42 II.

AS 42 Metropolitana

Another model, known as Saharan II or Metropolitana, was introduced in late 1943. Compared to the previous version, it had some changes: it did not have the top two rows of gasoline canisters on the sides, which were replaced by two large ammunition containers, and it had a folding cover. In addition, this version was equipped with Pirelli "Artiglio" tires, ideal for continental terrain, unlike the first model, which used Pirelli "Libya" sand tires.

Entering service in December 1942, the vehicle participated in the final stages of the campaign in Africa, particularly in operations in Libya and Tunisia. It was mainly assigned to the Saharan auto-avio companies of the Saharan "Mannerini" Regiment and the 103rd Arditi Truck Company of the 1st Special Arditi Battalion. The 2nd Battalion of the 10th Armored Regiment used it for the defense of Sicily and southern Italy. The same battalion, together with the Motorized Assault Battalion, employed both the "Saharans" and "Metropolitana" in the defense of Rome on Sept. 8, 1943. At the time of the armistice, the truck companies were disbanded, except for a group of 46 Arditi from the 10th Regiment, which, with 7-9 AS42s, joined the German 2. Fallschirmjäger-Division, to carry out reconnaissance missions on the Russian and French fronts, as well as in Belgium and the Netherlands. Some vehicles were also recovered and used by the "Barbarigo" Battalion of the 10th MAS Flotilla.

A dozen or so "Metropolitana," assigned to the Italian Africa Police after the war, were integrated into the Celeri and Mobile Departments of Public Security, where they remained in service until the mid-1950s.

▲ The SPA-Viberti AS42 'Metropolitana' truck 'Regio Esercito 1197B' licence plate, partially camouflaged with branches. On board RSI Arditi wearing the grey-green uniform while on the ground another pair of German Arditi and paratroopers can be seen. (Fallaok F1675 L37 - Werner Röpke- ECPAD - Défense).

AUTOPROTETTO S37, ITALY 1941-45

▲ Autoprotetto S37 troop carrier operating in the Balkans 1942-1943.

FIAT SPA S 37

■ THE ITALIAN ARMY'S ARMORED TROOP CARRIER

The Fiat-SPA Autoprotetto S37 was an armored troop transport vehicle developed and produced by the Società Piemontese Automobili (SPA). This vehicle was used by the Royal Italian Army during World War II, mainly in patrol and territorial control operations in the occupied Balkans.

■ DEVELOPMENT AND OPERATIONAL DEPLOYMENT

Development of the Autoprotetto S37 began in 1941, based on the chassis of the Libya version of the Fiat-SPA TL37 light artillery tractor. The project aimed to create an armored vehicle capable of transporting infantry more safely than other unprotected vehicles.

In 1942, the Royal Army acquired a total of 150 units, employing them mainly in security and anti-partisan combat tasks in the occupied territories of Yugoslavia and the Balkans. Because of its relatively light armor, the S37 was not suitable for the main front, but proved useful for garrison and patrol operations. Numerous were the specific units and departments of the Royal Army equipped with the S37 including:

- 31st Tank Regiment
- 955th and 1034th self-protected sections.
- 1118th Mixed Autosection of the "Macerata" Division
- 259th Self-protected Autoreparto
- LXXI Motorcycle Battalion, composed of elements of the 6th Bersaglieri Regiment

▲ Photo of a self-protected shielded S37 in use by the Italian army in Yugoslavia. The nine men in the squad are well armed, with at least two Breda model 1930 machine guns.

AUTOPROTETTO S37 GERMAN USE, 1942

▲ Autoprotetto S37 troop transporter captured and reused by the Germans after September 1943 and operated in the Balkans, 1943-45.

After the armistice of September 8, 1943, 37 examples fell into the hands of German forces, which integrated them into their own units and renamed them *Gepanzerte Manntransportwagen S 37* (italien) or, in abbreviated form, gep.M.Trsp.Wg. S37 250(i). Other vehicles, however, were captured and used by Yugoslav partisans.

Technical characteristics and armament

The self-protected S37 featured an open-top design, with the transport compartment protected by sloping armored panels bolted to the base frame, which retained the four-wheel-drive, steerable configuration of the TL37 tractor.

The vehicle could accommodate a total of 9 men, including the driver, who sat on a right front seat, and 8 infantrymen arranged on side benches inside the transport compartment. Access was through a split rear hatch.

Armament

The standard armament of the S37 consisted of an 8 mm Breda Mod. 38 machine gun mounted on a vehicle mount. However, other weapons were installed in some configurations, including:
- A flamethrower (for anti-partisan repression missions)
- One 47/32 Mod. 1935 anti-tank gun.

Because the vehicle did not have slits for small-arms fire from the interior, shields/ribs with slits were added above the transport compartment to allow soldiers to fire without exposing themselves excessively.

Mobility and autonomy

One of the strengths of the S37 was its remarkable mobility, provided by its all-wheel drive and all-wheel steering system, which allowed for greater agility over rough terrain. In addition, the vehicle boasted a good range, making it suitable for long-range operations. Some examples were also equipped with a Magneti Marelli RF3 M radio, improving communication and coordination capabilities with other units. The self-protected S37 represents an interesting evolution of troop transport vehicles of the time, combining mobility and protection in one vehicle, albeit limited by light armor.

▲ Photo of a vehicle just produced by FIAT, the self-protected S37 with a new E.R. number plate.

DATA SHEET SPA AUTOPROTETTO S37	
Dimensions	4.95 length x 1.92 width x 1.8 height (in m)
Weight	4.7 to 5.3 tonnes plus 770 kg payload
Crew	1 pilot plus a platoon of eight soldiers
Entering and leaving service	1941-1945
Fuel capacity	300 l
Engine	SPA 18VT petrol version III, 4 cylinders, 4053 cc
Maximum speed	52 km/h on road
Autonomy	725 km
Power	67 HP
Armament	1/2 Breda Mod. 193 or 1938 8 mm machine gun
Alternative armament	1 L/32 47mm anti-tank gun or flamethrower
Traction	4-wheel drive and steering
Production	150
Users	Kingdom of Italy and the German Wehrmacht

▲ An overcrowded AS37, far more than the 9 men assigned by regulation. Vehicle in use by the Italian army in Yugoslavia in 1943. The unit's logo is that of a leaping ibex. The circular motif is the classic army metal badge bearing the manufacturer's name.

Operational deployment

Although designed and equipped to operate in hot desert environments intended to support campaigns in North Africa, the AS37 was never deployed in that theater of war. Instead, the vehicle was employed in Yugoslavia to counter partisans and for convoy escort activities. AS37s were assigned to different departments. Operations in Yugoslavia proved extremely challenging for the AS37s, resulting in significant losses. However, at the end of April 1943, 102 vehicles were still operational with the Italian forces. By the time of the armistice in September 1943, the number dropped further and many of these vehicles ended up in the hands of Yugoslav partisan forces or the Germans, who managed to recover 37 units. Under German control, the AS37s continued to be used for internal security in an increasingly unstable Yugoslavia. In service with the German Army, the vehicle, in addition to fighting partisans, was also used against Soviet and Bulgarian forces toward the end of the war. The AS37 served in the 7th SS-Freiwilligen-Gebirgs "Prinz-Eugen" division and in some Wehrmacht units.

▲ Nice picture from the Bundesarchiv showing some German soldiers emerging from the rear hatch of their AS37 to take up operational positions. Note also the old Regio Esercito plate, which probably indicates that the changeover to Germanic hands took place a short time ago.

AUTOBLINDO SPA VIBERTI AS 43 ITALY R.S.I., 1944-1945

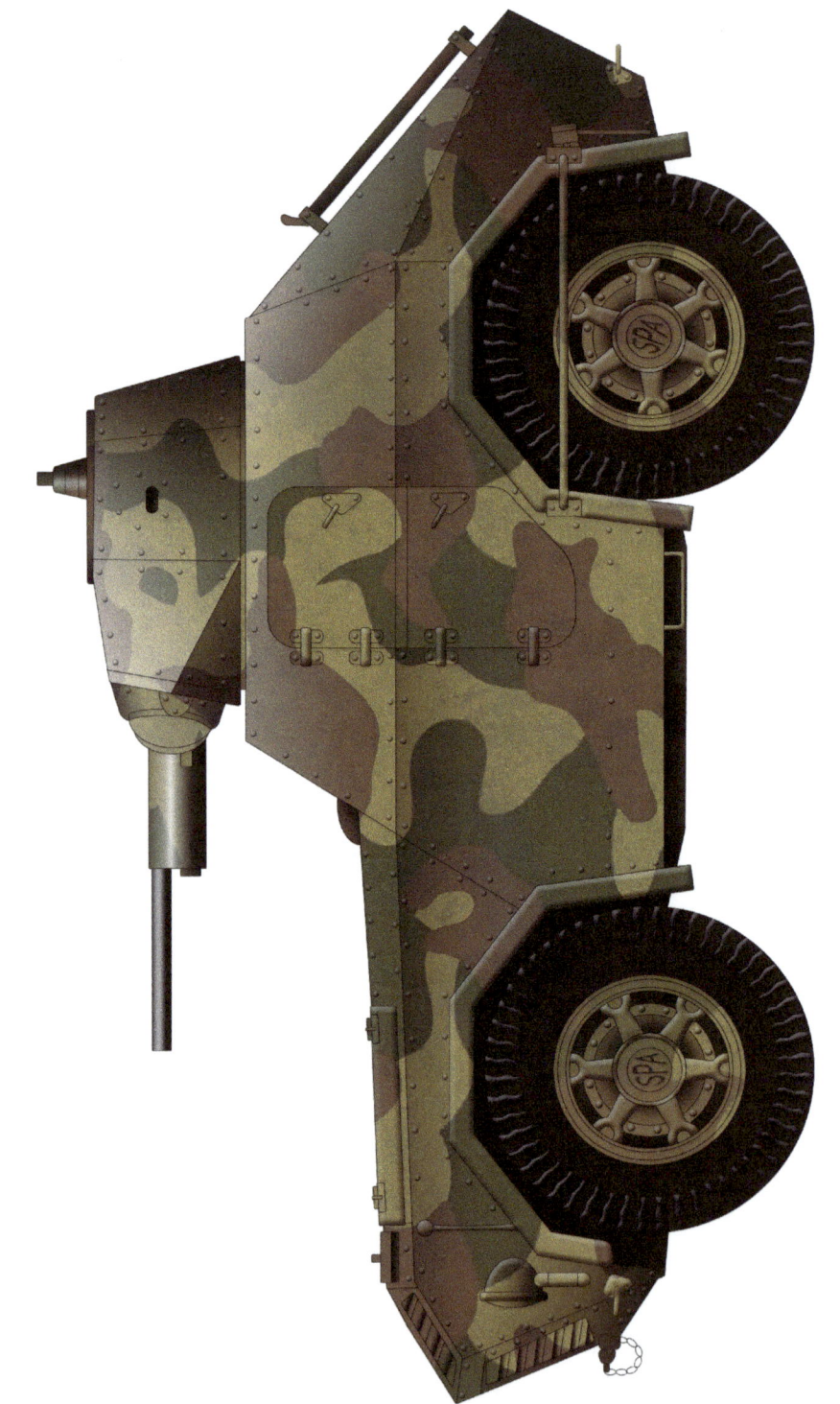

▲ Fiat Ansaldo AB41 armoured car in Libya. Belonging to the 3rd Armoured Group 'Nice', 1st squadron, 4th platoon, spring 1942, Libya.

SPA VIBERTI AS 43

SPA VIBERTI 43: AN EVOLUTION OF AS 42

The SPA Viberti 43, also known as **AS 43**, or also by the name *Carozzeria Speciale AS43* (depending on the manufacturer) was an armored car made by the Società Piemontese Automobili or SPA, a subsidiary of FIAT, and Officine Viberti , both based in Turin. The project was initiated using the chassis of the FIAT-SPA AS37 (AS for Saharan Truck) light truck, itself derived from the FIAT-SPA Light Tractor 37 'Libya'. The new armored car was produced in a very small run. Developed in 1943 to meet new tactical requirements that arose on the battlefield. The need for a stronger armored vehicle with superior armament capabilities prompted SPA Viberti to design a vehicle that could not only cope with the difficulties of the terrain but also compete with heavier enemy vehicles.

Project and Development

The SPA AS43 represented a military vehicle developed in response to the Republican Army's need for a reconnaissance and infantry support armored car that would be cheaper and easier to manufacture than the better-known AB40/41 and AB43 models already in use and derived from the Royal Army. This vehicle was designed and produced in 1944 by Viberti from the technical basis of the "Autoblindo Africa Settentrionale Italiana" (ABS37), a model already developed by the Società Piemontese Automobili. The ABS37, in turn, had been conceived in 1941 together with the S37 troop transport vehicle, the latter being the only one of the two models to have actually been adopted by the Royal Army. Both vehicles were based on the Fiat-SPA TL37 light artillery tractor chassis.

▲ Photo of an armoured AS43, taken inside the Officine Viberti factory in Turin. The hand tools on the back are not present, but the fuel tank cap is visible. Source: Viberti Archives.

The AS43 was armed with the turret of the AB40 armored car, which mounted a Breda Mod. 38 machine gun. This vehicle found use mainly among the fascist forces of the Italian Social Republic (RSI), particularly in the Black Brigades and the Republican National Guard. At least two examples were assigned to the Armored Group "Leonessa" of the Republican National Guard, which used them in operations to counter partisan resistance in Piedmont. The AS43, therefore, not only met specific tactical needs, but also fit into the broader context of the Italian Civil War, becoming an operational tool in the hands of Republican forces during the final years of the conflict.

▲ A Spa-Viberti AS43 in the Lamarma barracks during maintenance. A soldier is busy playing silence right in front of the vehicle. Source: wikipedia.

AUTOBLINDO SPA VIBERTI AS 43 G.N.R. ITALY R.S.I., 1944-1945

▲ AB42 armoured car. Developed only in prototype terms, it served essentially to refine the future AB43.

DATA SHEET SPA VIBERTI AS 43	
Dimensions	5 length x 1.9 width x 2.5 height (in m)
Weight	6,5 t
Crew	3: pilot, foreman and attendant
Entering and leaving service	1944-1945
Fuel capacity	120 l
Engine	SPA 18VT petrol, 4 cylinders, 4053 cc
Maximum speed	50 km/h on road
Autonomy	250 km
Power	67 HP
Armament	1 Breda 20/65 Mod. 1935 20 mm gun
Secondary armament	1 Breda mod 38
Traction	4-wheel drive and steering
Production	2 to 6 models
Users	Kingdom of Italy and the National Republican Army

▲ The two special vehicles on Spa-Viberti AS43 during the Armoured Group 'Leonessa' parade held in Turin on 23 May 1944. The two AS43s and the AB41 on the right are painted in Saharan khaki. The unit's coat of arms on the far left is clearly visible. Piazza Carlo Felice, near the Porta Nuova railway station. Source P. Crippa.

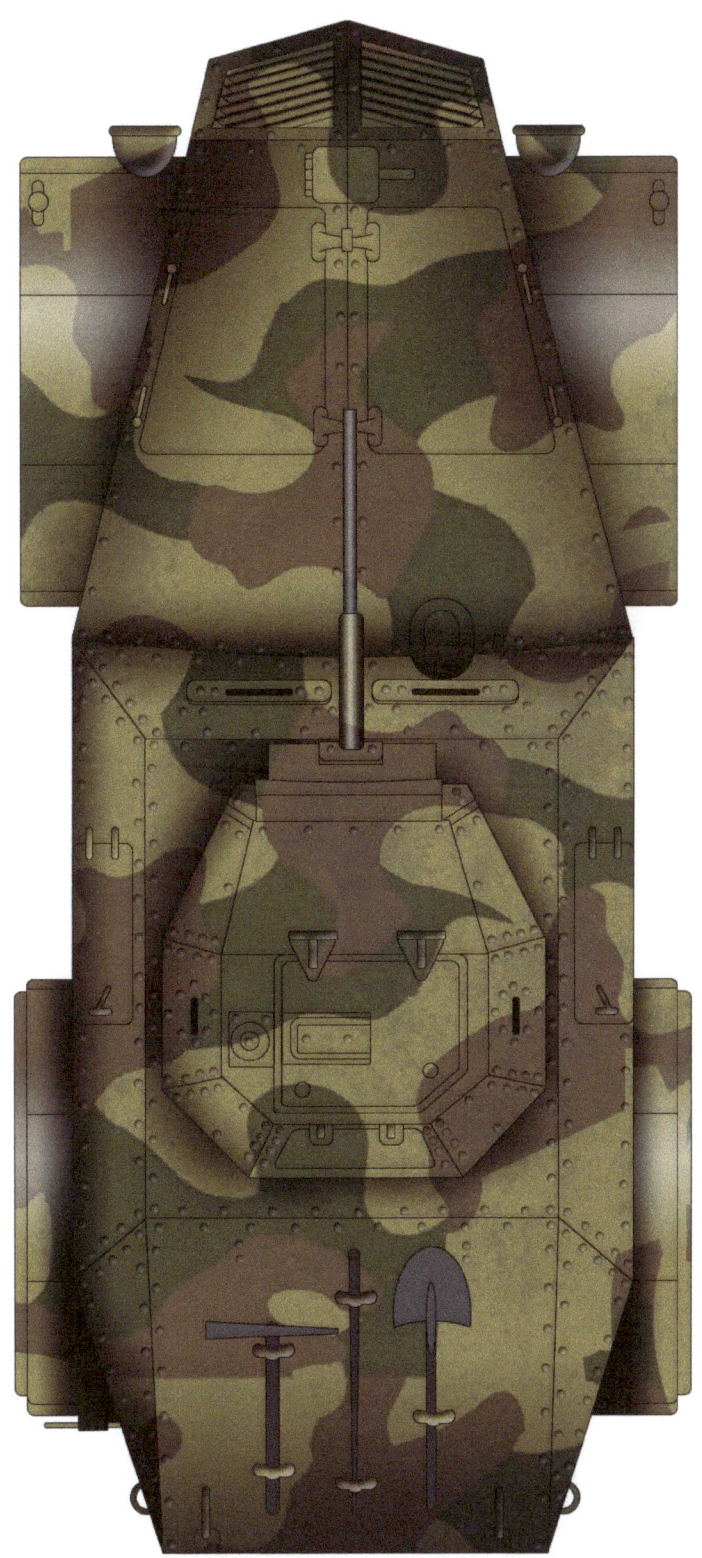

▲ AS 43 armoured car profile as seen from above.

▲ Armoured car profile AS 43 front and rear view.

Technical Characteristics

The hull of this "republican" Autoblinda traces in its lines that of the Autoprotetto S37. In the hull, accessed by a side hatch in two elements, take place the conductor and the servant.

The armament was all concentrated in the turret, which was entirely derived from the L6/40 light tank: the main weapon was thus the Breda 20/65 Mod. 1935 20-mm cannon-miter; the secondary weapon was the classic Breda Mod. 38 8-mm coaxial. Stowed in the combat compartment were 10 20-mm magazine boxes and 6 8-mm ammunition boxes.

Operational Employment

Many Italian sources claim that Paolo Zerbino, Head of the Province of Turin from October 21, 1943 to May 7, 1944 and later Minister of the Interior of the Italian Social Republic, "participated" in the development of the SPA-Viberti AS43. Although little is known about production dates, it is likely that the first two examples were produced by May 1944. They were first spotted on May 23, 1944 in a parade of the 'Leonessa' Armored Group in Turin. The first vehicles were assigned to Armored Group 'Leonessa', stationed near Montichiari, near Brescia in Lombardy.

In late February or early March 1944, the unit was transferred to Turin, Piedmont, and employed almost exclusively in anti-partisan roles for the remainder of the war. The two companies were stationed in the Caserma Dabormida and Caserma La Marmora barracks in Turin.

In the summer of 1944, the unit was employed in hunting partisans between the provinces of Ivrea and Biella in northern Piedmont. A total of 33 partisans were captured in these raids, as well as 3 Australian soldiers who escaped from a prison camp and some military equipment.

In June 1944, the 'Leonessa' Armored Group, thanks to the continuous flow of volunteers, grew and strengthened, and was now composed of: 1st Tank Company, 2nd Armored Car Company and 3rd Armored Company. Toward the end of April 1945, a detachment of the group, also consisting of at least two armored cars, AS43, was sent to Valtellina, near Tirano in Lombardy, with the task of keeping the area free of partisans. In what the secretary of the Italian Fascist Party, Alessandro Pavolini, renamed the "Republican Alpine Redoubt."

Later, towards the end of April, all of the Leonessa divisions remaining in Turin came under continuous and constant pressure from the many partisans active in the city, and eventually they too were forced to leave the Piedmontese capital, reaching in turn the Valtellina redoubt. Here they joined with the rest of the black brigades assigned there, some 10,000 men, until all of them surrendered to the Anglo-Americans on May 5, 1945. The last noteworthy battle was the so-called Battle of Titan on April 27, in which the last AS43 also ended up captured by the partisans.

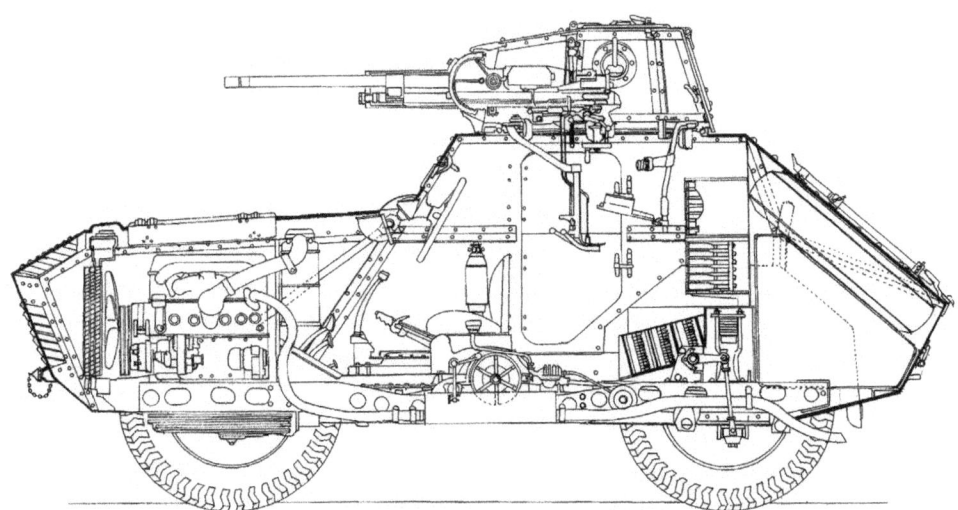

▲ X-ray diagram of the AS43 showing the inside of the combat chamber, engine compartment and spaces for stowing ammunition. Source: Viberti Archives.

CAMIONETTA AS 43 DESERTICA, ITALY 1943

▲ AS43 truck in camouflage version, armed with Breda 20/65 Model 1935 anti-aircraft machine gun. Rome, Italy, late summer 1943.

CAMIONETTA AS 43 DESERTICA

AS 43 DESERTICA: DESIGNED FOR THE DESERT

The SPA-Viberti AS43 was an Italian reconnaissance vehicle designed for the Royal Army, intended primarily for long-range reconnaissance missions in the North African desert, designed to cope with the extreme conditions of the desert, where fine sand and rough terrain tested the mobility and reliability of armored vehicles. Its tasks included organizing ambushes against Allied convoys, countering Long Range Desert Group (LRDG) operations, and escorting Axis convoys along desert routes. However, the vehicle was introduced too late to take an active part in the North African campaign. As a result, it was used exclusively in Italy and the Balkan region. It is remembered as a baptism of fire, the desperate defense of Rome in September 1943.

Project and Development

The Officine Viberti design team, inspired by reports regarding various pre-existing trucks, began developing a new reconnaissance vehicle based on the chassis of the FIAT-SPA Autocarri Sahariani Model 1937 or AS37 light truck. It is likely that the project was influenced during its development phase by reports about the AS37 Light Truck received in the summer of 1942 from the Libyan Sahara Military Command. Toward the end of that summer, the prototype of the new vehicle, initially called the SPA-Viberti AS43 Desert Camionetta, was presented at the Centro Studi ed Esperienze della Motorizzazione in Rome. This prototype was distinguished from the production models by the presence on the sides of two 20-liter jerry can holders, allowing the transport of a total of 10 jerry cans. However, after the loss of North Africa, the mass-produced vehicles underwent modifications: the jerrycan holders were removed and the free space was converted into lockers for ammunition storage.

Technical characteristics

The Model 1943 Desert Truck, a light truck designed for the desert, was equipped with a FIAT-SPA Type 18TL gasoline engine, a water-cooled inline four-cylinder capable of delivering 52 hp at 2,000 rpm. The

▲ A patrol of the Regio Esercito's Formation Group 'A' on an AS43 desert truck, testing at the Centro Studi ed Esperienze della Motorizzazione in Rome. Regio Esercito number plate 36749.

engine's maximum speed was limited to 2,000 rpm to prolong its operational life, thus reducing the need for maintenance and associated costs. The Zenith Model 1936 TTHVI carburetor was specifically designed to ensure reliable performance in off-road conditions and on sloping terrain.

The FIAT-SPA TL37 tractor also mounted the same engine. In the vehicles destined for Libya, the Zenith air filter had been replaced with an oil-bath OCI model, which was better suited to desert conditions.

The engine-clutch assembly was attached to the chassis through four silent block mounts, providing greater stability and reduced vibration during operation.

▲ Italian crew belonging to the republican army (GNR) struggling with their AS43 armoured truck.

CAMIONETTA AS 43 DESERTICA, 1943

▲ AS43 truck in troop-transport version, armed with Breda 8mm light machine gun Mod. 38. Italy, 1943.

CAMIONETTA AS 43 DESERTICA, ITALY 1943

▲ AS43 truck in camouflage version with rear side reinforcements, armed with Breda 20/65 Model 1935 cannon. Italy 1943.

Truck armament

The main armament of the SPA-Viberti AS43 truck consisted of a Breda 20/65 Model 1935 automatic antiaircraft gun, manufactured by the Società Italiana Ernesto Breda per Costruzioni Meccaniche. Although designed for the antiaircraft role, it could also be used effectively against light armored vehicles, such as reconnaissance tanks or armored cars.

In its field configuration, the cannon required a five-man crew, but aboard the truck the staff was reduced to three: a gunner and two loaders. The gunner operated the cannon from a rear position, while the two servants sat on either side of the gun in the hold. The driver could occasionally assist in loading to speed up the firing cadence.

The weapon had a maximum range of 1,500-2,000 meters against aerial targets and as much as 5,000 meters against ground targets, with an effective range reduced, however, to about 2,500 meters. Considered one of the best light automatic weapons of its era, it weighed a total of 330 kg and could theoretically fire up to 500 rounds per minute. However, the effective firing rate was reduced to about 300 rounds per minute if the gun was fed from a single magazine. The maximum depression angle was -10°, while the elevation reached +80°.

As a secondary weapon, the truck was equipped with a Breda Model 1937 medium machine gun mounted on a gooseneck mount on the left side of the cab. This machine gun was employed by the commander to fire at enemy infantry or low-flying aircraft.

▲ Column of AS43s outside the SPA Viberti workshops, in camouflage colour, ready to be sent to operational departments. Pictured top left: the crew of the Breda 20mm machine gun housed by the AS43 truck. In the small photo on the right: an AS43 being supplied to the Whermacht divisions.

DATA SHEETCAMIONETTA AS 43 DESERTICA	
Dimensions	4.65 length x 2 width x 2.70 height (in m)
Weight	5 t
Crew	5 (pilot, commander, gunner and 2 attendants)
Entering and leaving service	1943
Fuel capacity	150 l
Engine	SPA 18VT petrol engine, 4 cylinders, 4053 cc.
Maximum speed	50 km/h on road
Autonomy	900 km
Power	52 HP
Armament	1 Breda 20/65 Model 1935 gun
Secondary armament	A Breda Model 1937 Medium Machine Gun
Traction	4-wheel drive and steering
Production	11 conversions for desert, N.A. for AS 43 post-September 43
Users	Kingdom of Italy and National Republican Army, Germany.

▶ Another beautiful picture of the AS43 on patrol of the Regio Esercito's Formation Group 'A' desert truck AS43, in testing at the Centro Studi ed Esperienze della Motorizzazione in Rome.

▲ AS43 truck in camouflaged armoured version with rear side reinforcements, armed with one or two Breda mm Model 1938 machine guns. Italy 1945.

AUTOBLINDO LANCIA "LINCE"

■ LINCE: A SUSTAINABLE AND FLEXIBLE VEHICLE

The Autoblindo Lince was a reconnaissance vehicle employed by the Italian Social Republic and the German army in the period 1943-1945, during World War II. And again until the mid-1950s also by the police departments of the new Italian republic. It was a replica of the British Daimler Dingo, models of which were captured by the Italians in the North African campaigns. Like its enemy equivalent, the Lince was used mainly for reconnaissance missions. It was equipped with an 8 mm Breda 38 machine gun as its only armament. A total of 392 examples were produced, including 263 by Lancia and 129 by Ansaldo. In the German armed forces, the vehicle was identified as Panzerspähwagen Lince 202(i).

Project and Development

Made in collaboration between Lancia Veicoli Industriali and Ansaldo, the Lince was designed to meet the speed and maneuverability needs of Italian troops engaged on the North African front and in other theaters of operation. In 1941, the Italian Ministry of War requested Lancia to develop a chassis that would be able to accommodate an armored body, equipped with some advanced features. The specifications called for the vehicle to be equipped with a four-wheel all-wheel drive and to be able to maintain high speed over difficult terrain, features critical for operations in African deserts and reconnaissance missions. High-acceleration independent suspension was also a priority to ensure that the vehicle was capable of dealing with rough terrain without compromising speed performance.

Lancia, in collaboration with Ansaldo, was inspired by a design that was similar to that of the British Daimler Scout Car, better known as the Daimler Dingo, a light vehicle that the Italians had captured in

▲ A front view of a production Lancia Lince Autoblinda at the Ansaldo-Fossati factory. Note also the typical camouflage adopted in 1943 by the RSI.

AUTOBLINDO "LINCE" ITALY, RSI 1943-1945

▲ Lancia/Ansaldo armoured car 'Lince' in the armoured group 'M' Leonessa, of the Guardia NazinaleRepubblicana in Piacenza, R.S.I, Italy, April 1945.

AUTOBLINDO AS42, S37, AS43, AS43 ARMOURED CAR & LINCE

DATA SHEET AUTOBLINDO "LINCE"	
Dimensions	3.2 length x 1.75 width x 1.65 height (in m)
Weight	3.1 tonnes fully loaded
Crew	2 (pilot and weapon commander)
Entering and leaving service	1942-1955
Fuel capacity	150 l
Engine	Lancia Astura 8-cylinder V-twin 2,617 cm^3
Maximum speed	85 km/h on road
Autonomy	350 km
Power	60 HP
Armament	A Breda 8mm-calibre Model 38 machine gun
Armouring	Front 14 mm; side 8.5 mm
Traction	4-wheel drive and steering
Production	392: 263 by Lancia and 129 by Ansaldo
Users	National Republican Army, German Army, Italian Republic

Libya and which represented, in the eyes of the Italian General Staff an ideal example of a light and agile vehicle for reconnaissance operations. The Lince prototype was then unveiled in November 1942 and showed a great and almost identical resemblance to the Daimler Dingo, but with some technical modifications to adapt it to Italian specifications.

The first examples were made in 1943, with production to continue until 1944, but in relatively small numbers compared to other Italian armored cars of the time. Total production amounted to about 390 examples, intended mainly for reconnaissance units and armored troops.

▲ The very cramped interior of the Lince armoured car could accommodate a maximum of two people.

AUTOBLINDO "LINCE" ITALY, POLICE CORPS, 1945-1945

▲ Lancia/Ansaldo 'Lince' armoured car used by Italian police units of the 2nd Celere Division, 1945-1955.

AUTOBLINDO "LINCE" GERMAN USE 1943-1945

▲ Lancia/Ansaldo 'Lince' armoured car used by Wermacht units, 1943-1945.

▲ Lancia/Ansaldo 'Lince' armoured car captured and in the possession of Wermacht units under the name Panzerspahwagen Lince 202(i), 1945.

Technical Characteristics

The Lince retained the Fiat 18A engine, but its main feature was its ability to operate in complex scenarios, both desert and mountainous, thanks to its advanced suspension system that improved stability. The vehicle mounted a Breda 38 machine gun and, in some cases, heavier armament such as a 20 mm cannon. The vehicle was equipped with the engine of the Lancia Astura, modified to increase engine torque. The gearbox was equipped with a hydraulic preselector, inspired by the British model, as were the transmissions and suspension. A noteworthy feature was the presence of all four steering wheels, which provided greater maneuverability.

The bodywork as mentioned, traced that of the British armored vehicle, except for the rear, where the engine was located. Compared to Italian-made armored cars, this version was distinguished by welded armor, unlike other Italian armored cars, which used shaped armor plates attached with tapered bolts or, in some cases, studded on a frame.

▲ Two curious uses of the Lince armoured car. Left: a vehicle that ended up in the hands of partisan formations towards the end of the war. Right: a 'Lince' drives a column of a celere department of the Italian State Police in 1950.

▼ Two Italian soldiers in Libya supported the captured British Auoblindo Damler Dingo, progenitor of the Lince.

AUTOBLINDO OPERATIONAL USE

The AS 42 Autoblinda, the SPA Viberti 43, the AS 43 Desertica and the Lince played a decisive role in different phases of World War II, particularly during the campaigns in North Africa, the Axis front and operations on the Eastern Front and in the period after September 1943. Each version of the vehicle was designed to meet specific tactical and environmental requirements, thus providing crucial operational flexibility for Italian and Axis forces. This chapter examines the operational use of these vehicles in major military campaigns, highlighting the different phases of the war, the difficulties encountered and the successes achieved.

THE CAMPAIGN OF NORTH AFRICA (1940-1943)

The North African Campaign, fought between 1940 and 1943, represented one of the most important theaters of war of World War II, in which Axis forces composed of Italians and Germans clashed with Allied forces in an extremely difficult environment. AS 42 armored cars, in particular, proved to be strategic assets in reconnaissance, patrolling and ground troop support operations. The desert environment, with its fine sand, extremely high temperatures and poor cover, necessitated the design of highly specialized vehicles.

The First Use of AS 42 in the Desert
The AS 42 was first deployed in 1941, when the Italian army began to gain experience on the desert terrain in North Africa. This armored vehicle was mainly used in reconnaissance operations and patrols against Allied forces. Its ability to cover large distances in the desert, thanks to the speed and mobility offered by the Fiat 18A engine, made it particularly useful for obtaining strategic information on the movement of enemy forces and for launching rapid attacks against vulnerable enemy units.
The AS 42 armored cars were distinguished by their speed and armored protection, which made them resilient against enemy small arms, but limitations were evident when heavier targets such as tanks or Allied anti-tank guns were encountered. Initially, the AS 42 was successful in long-range reconnaissance operations, but its mobility in sandy terrain and difficulty in dealing with Allied armored forces led to the evolution of later versions.

The Introduction of AS 42 Saharan
The most iconic version of the AS 42 in the context of the North African campaign was the **AS 42 Saharan**, which was developed specifically to operate in the desert. The AS 42 Saharan had the same basic features as the AS 42, but with crucial modifications, such as wider tires and an upgraded suspension, which allowed the vehicle to move more easily in the sand without getting stuck. In addition, armament was upgraded, with the ability to mount machine guns or 20 mm cannons, which enabled the Saharan to fight enemy light vehicles and offer fire support to Italian forces engaged on the ground. In 1941, the AS 42 Sahariana stood out for its use in disruptive operations against Allied supply lines. Its characteristics allowed rapid raids and equally rapid retreats, avoiding involvement in prolonged engagements with enemy forces superior in numbers and armament. The Saharan was also used in long-range patrol and reconnaissance missions, as well as serving as support to larger ground forces, such as in invasion offensives in Libya and Tunisia, where its use as a fast attack vehicle proved decisive in some partial successes against Allied lines.

The Desert Version (AS 43 Desert)
The **AS 43 Desertica** version was also designed to meet the specific needs of the desert; its ability to traverse sandy terrain, combined with a powerful 125-horsepower engine, made it suitable for traveling the long distances between supply lines and battlefronts, while improved armor protection made it more resistant to small arms and explosions. However, due to developments in the war it did not find use in the context of the African campaigns. The AS43 thus played an important role in the RSI and the Wehrmacht after September 1943.

THE SICILY CAMPAIGN AND THE INVASION OF ITALY (1943)

In 1943, with the invasion of Sicily and the subsequent invasion of the Italian peninsula, armored vehicles such as the AS 42 and its variants played a significant role in defensive operations, but also in supporting Italian troops trying to slow the Allied advance.

The Role of Sahariana in Sicily
The Sahariana was among the vehicles that continued to be used in southern Italy, especially during the final phase of the campaign in Sicily, where Italian forces were trying to counter the Allied invasion. Its speed and mobility enabled it to carry out rapid attacks against Allied support forces, although the Allies' numerical and technological superiority in Sicily was now overwhelming. The Saharan was mainly involved in reconnaissance missions and raids against supply lines, but it was not enough to prevent the Allied advance.

AS 43 in Southern Italy
The AS 43 and its variants also continued to be employed in defensive battles against the Allied invasion, but scarcity of supplies and depletion of resources gradually reduced their effectiveness. Their use was mainly concentrated in rear-guard operations, protecting Italian and German retreats by attempting to slow the enemy advance. However, increasing Allied pressure and the effectiveness of Allied armored vehicles gradually reduced the number of operational vehicles of the Axis forces.

◄ ▼ Two beautiful archive images of Italian soldiers on desert reconnaissance patrols with their Saharan AS 42s. The men appear in a warlike pose probably for army propaganda offices to show the armament of this certainly interesting vehicle.

▲ Various pictures of AS42 Sahariana made with Italeri models by Paolo Crippa of Milan and others.

■ THE CAMPAIGN IN GREECE, THE BALKANS AND ON THE EAST FRONT (1941-1944)

Although the main employment of the last Italian armored cars was concentrated in North Africa, some models were also employed in the Greek Campaign and some even in operations on the Eastern Front, where climatic and land conditions required desert-like solutions.

The Role of SPA Viberti 43 on the Eastern Front.
Axis forces, engaged against the Red Army, needed vehicles that could operate in rugged environments, such as forests and frozen plains. The SPA Viberti 43 was primarily employed for flanking operations, attempting to penetrate Soviet territory to disrupt enemy supply lines and inflict damage on rear guards. Some pictures of the AS42 show this vehicle engaged on the Ukrainian front on pages 17 and 20.

Conclusions
The operational use of armored vehicles such as the AS 42 and other armored cars and trucks in the various campaigns of World War II demonstrates the great adaptability of these vehicles to the requirements of modern warfare. Improved versions, such as the Sahariana and SPA Viberti 43, marked the evolution of the Italian forces as they sought to respond to the challenges posed by their enemies. Despite the increasing superiority of the Allied forces, Italian armored cars remained instruments of great strategic importance, performing reconnaissance, support and defense functions until the final stages of the conflict. Modifications made to each model helped improve the operational capabilities of Italian forces and solidified the reputation of Italian armored vehicles during World War II.

▲ The SPA-Viberti AS43 Truck. Source: War History Museum Collection.

▲ ► Profiles of the main weapons used on the armoured cars presented in this volume. Above and right: the complex profile of the Breda 20/65 Model 1935 automatic anti-aircraft gun, produced by the Società Italiana Ernesto Breda per Costruzioni Meccaniche.

▼ Below: the 'Elefantino' 47/32 mod. 1935 anti-tank gun.

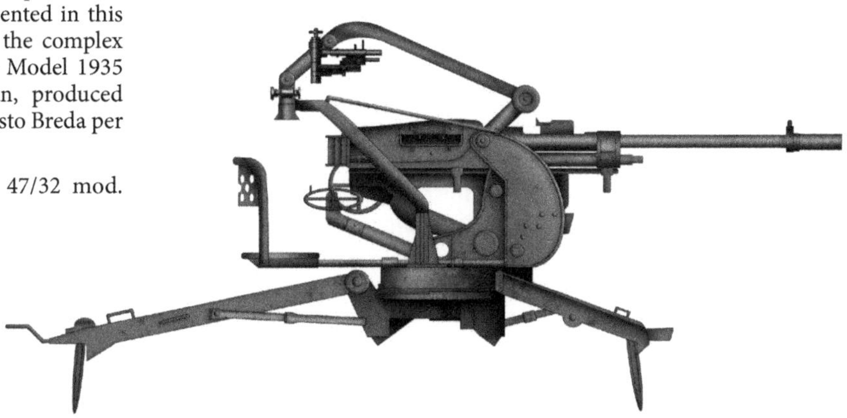

AUTOBLINDO AS42, S37, AS43, AS43 ARMOURED CAR & LINCE

CAMOUFLAGE AND MARKINGS

The background colors of the Autoblindos, from their creation until 1945, (the operational period of such use is indicated in brackets) used, moreover, also for all armored vehicles were: gray-green R.E. (1936-1945), dark chocolate (1936-1941), reddish brown (1936-1943), ochre (for prototypes), sand (1941-1945), dark sand (1943-1945), dark gray (1941-1943). Medium green (1936-1943) and dark red (for prototypes) were used for camouflage.

National territory 1936-1940-substantial prevalence of gray-green.
Occupation of Albania and the French Front 1939-1940 - gray-green.
Greece and Yugoslavia campaign 1940-1941 - gray-green possibly camouflaged with green and sand-colored speckles.
East Africa 1940-1941 - gray green or in old Ethiopian campaign camouflage reddish brown with green spots.
North Africa 1940-1943 - at first only gray green, color with which they were generally landed at destination ports, then sand color in various variegated versions. Not used in the Russian Campaign 1941-1943.
RSI 1943-1945 gray-green, dark sand yellow, reddish brown color with dense medium green speckling, in uniform color German panzer grey. In particular, dark sand color were the wagons of the "Leonessa" and to some extent the "Leoncello" and "San Giusto." I also report the presence of elaborate camouflage in irregular checkerboard patterns of sandy yellow background and green and brown patches.
Police Corps until 1952 dark brick red background color.
Specific armored car camouflage: the prototypes were painted at the factory with a so-called "imperial" livery that consisted of a series of relatively thin dark green and dark brown streaks applied over a background of light Saharan khaki known as sand color in Italy. This livery was never adopted for production examples, which were instead painted a slightly lighter shade of Saharan khaki than that used for armored vehicles. If destined for Africa the vehicles appear to have remained in their color scheme or repainted once they reached their destination in similar colors, while in vehicles for continental use they often wore factory-applied or circumstantial camouflage schemes. Instead, the last AB 41s and most of the AB 43s left the factory with a somewhat complex three-tone camouflage livery involving green and reddish-brown patches interspersed with sand-colored streaks.

■ MEDIUM, LIGHT AND ARMORED CAR BADGES

In order to recognize individual armored vehicles in military operations, even for Italy, it became necessary to introduce an identification system, partly because at least initially there were no tanks with radio equipment installed. In fact, radios did not begin to be installed with any regularity until 1941. At first, flags with red or white drapes were used to communicate.
The first table of distinctive vehicle markings dates back to 1925 and was very complex and articulated

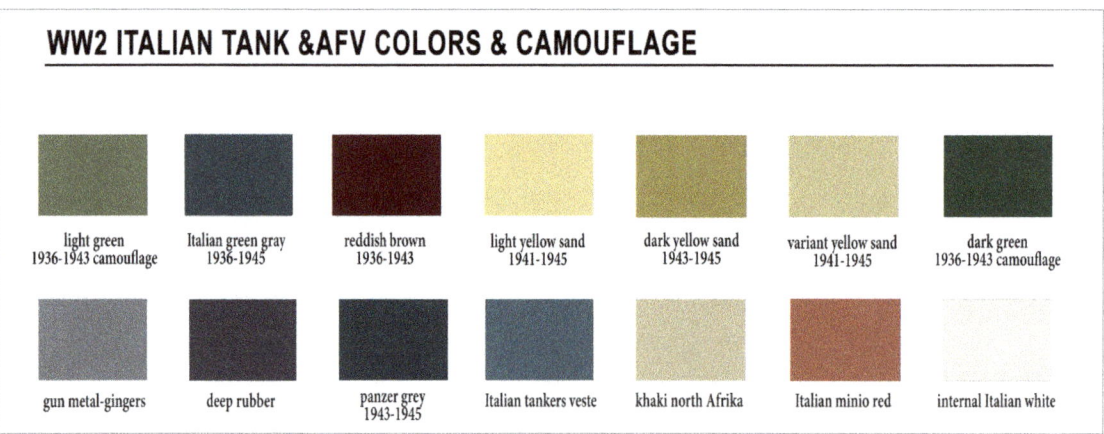

to excess. The numerical groups were not introduced until 1927 after the establishment of the Tank Regiment; new regulations were then issued in 1928. In 1940 the first deliveries of M13/40 Wagons finally began and were distributed to the various armored units.

The armored cars, as had been the case with the Medium or Light tanks, bore symbols identified by markings, names and numbers placed on the sides of the hull on both sides. The numbers were painted frontally on the hull plate and on both sides.

In 1938, to simplify their recognition, another change was made, this time a radical one: new tactical symbols were established for the tanks. System that the armored cars born a few years later then also followed. The companies of the vehicles were represented by colored rectangles in the following manner: The first company had the color red, the 2$^{(}$a) blue, the 3$^{(a)}$ yellow, and the 4^a green; the color white was reserved for the regimental command vehicles. he insignia of the tanks and armored cars had to be 20 x 12 cm in size and painted in paint of the company color.

The colored rectangles were cut by white bars (1 to 4 rows and a diagonal for 5th Platoon) and indicated the different platoons, full color and without rows for Company Command wagons.

The rectangles of the various platoons were surmounted by an Arabic number (the color of the company) indicative of the vehicle in the platoon's organic formation.

These numbers were to be 10 cm high and 1.5 cm thick, and placed in the center of the upper side of the rectangle 2 cm apart. Below the rectangle, however, the number of the battalion to which it belonged was placed in white Roman numerals. Battalion wagons, if in reserve at the Regimental level carried, however, only the relative Arabic number. Battalion command squadron wagons had a completely black rectangle. The battalion command vehicle on two companies had it half red and half blue (right). The battalion command vehicle on three companies had it on three colored lines from left to right: red, blue and yellow. Specifically on the medium wagons, the distinctive sign was placed on the turret in the front middle-high part. Posteriorly, in the middle part of the turret. On some wagons the rectangle was placed at the height of the hatchway to the combat chamber. On the same hatch, the distinctive sign of the Division, such as a black ram, also often appeared. The medium-sized wagons used by the Italian Social Republic showed the distinctive signs of the various divisions painted on them: the "Leoncello" was depicted by a black lion clutching a fascio littorio looking to the left on a white background. The "Leonessa" had a somewhat more complicated insignia formed by the red M of Mussolini, cut by a black-colored bundle and underneath the also black inscription "GNR."

The vehicles used by the Germans, especially those captured, and the new ones ordered, after the armistice in 1943 bore the typical German army markings starting with the black and white *Ritterkreuz* in its various fashions.

Specifically for armored cars on Regulation No. 4640 it was reported that:
- The distinctive mark should have been affixed in the turret, at the figure center of the rear plate and laterally--right and left--at the figure center of the plates adjacent to the front plate;
- The Roman and Arabic numbers indicative of the Gr. Sqd (or Btg.) and Rgt. Should be affixed to the right side of the rear plate of the combat booth, in the center of figure of the surface, right and left, respectively, of the retreating machine gun.

Despite the fact that this regulation prescribed how, "Other badges (call sign, numerical group, etc.) on the outside of the wagons, other than those strictly prescribed by regulatory provisions are prohibited."

In reality things turned out differently, and in fact free interpretations of the regulations were adopted. Such badges were still carried on the sides of the superstructure and at the front on the fender. In Africa such badges were often carried larger to ensure greater visibility. In addition, as was already the case for tanks, again in Africa, starting in 1941 it became mandatory to adopt devices for aerial recognition that for the AB, which was the customary white circle 70 cm. in diameter painted externally on the turret top. Prior to this expedient, as well indicated in some of the pictures relating to "Nice" armored cars and other Italian vehicles mistakenly ran into attacks by our planes and bombers or the Axis in general. At first they resorted to huge colored tricolor flags on the front and side vehicles and then switched to the aforementioned white circle.

PRODUCTION AND EXPORT

The export of Italian armored vehicles, particularly the Autoblinda AS 42 and other last-generation armored cars or trucks such as the SPA Viberti 43, and the AS 43 Desertica, represented an important aspect of the Italian war industry during and after World War II. Although production was primarily intended to meet the needs of the Italian armed forces, a significant portion of the vehicles were exported to allied and neutral countries and, in some cases, to nations under Axis influence. Many as usual ended up in German hands following the Italian disruption during the armistice in September 1943.

■ MAIN RECIPIENTS OF EXPORT

The export of Italian vehicles took place in a very delicate geopolitical context, with Italy committed to supporting its strategic alliances and strengthening its international position. **The AS 42 armored cars** and other more advanced versions were mainly directed to recipients such as Spain, the Balkans, the RSI and partisan forces, and some other Mediterranean nations.

Franco's Spain

Francoist Spain represented one of the main buyers of Italian armored vehicles before and during World War II. Although Spain was not directly involved in the conflict alongside the Axis forces, it maintained a close relationship with Fascist Italy, especially in the procurement of military equipment. Beginning in 1941, Spain received a significant amount of armored vehicles, including the AS 42 and its modified version, the Sahariana, which was well suited to the needs of the Spanish desert and rough terrain. These vehicles were used mainly in patrol and border defense operations, as well as in support of police and anti-partisan operations within Iberian territory.

Nazi Germany

During World War II, **Germany** was one of Italy's main allies until 1943, and again after that with the RSI in northern Italy, and played a crucial role in the procurement and distribution of war vehicles. Although Germany had its own production of armored vehicles, the escalation of the conflict led the German power to use any type of vehicle captured from the enemies, or as in the case of Italy to confiscate a large number of vehicles of the Royal Army following its collapse after September 1943. These included, of course, the armored cars that are the subject of this study. Italian armored cars were prized by the Wehrmacht for their **versatility** and **reliability** in difficult terrain such as the desert. Vehicles captured by the Germans and deployed by the Luftwaffe were generally refueled/upgraded with German ordnance. The 2-cm FlaK 38 20-mm anti-aircraft machine gun was mounted on the platform, while the 7.92-mm Mauser 7.92-caliber MG 15 aviation machine gun was used for close defense.

However, limited domestic production and resource scarcity during the conflict prevented a large deployment of Italian vehicles in German forces.

The CSR and the partisan forces

A large part of these weapons, made around the middle of the conflict, ended up playfully in the hands of that state that was born out of the ashes of the Italian army after the aforementioned armistice of 1043, namely the Italian Social Republic. The Salo authorities, in close cooperation with the Germanic forces in Italy acquired a number of Italian vehicles to strengthen their armed forces. All the last Italian armored cars and trucks were used both for the protection of internal infrastructure and for support of operations against partisan forces. These vehicles were used to control rural areas although their effectiveness was limited by the ongoing conflict and logistical difficulties.

For the same reason with the approaching end of the conflict and the subsequent collapse of the Italian-German forces, many of these weapons ended up falling into the hands of the partisan forces.

The End of World War II and Postwar Export.

With the end of the war, and the related reassignment in the western sphere of Italy, many weapons of the type of armored cars were used mainly in the Police on Italian territory, remaining active, as in the case of the Lince and AS43 until the 1950s.

After the war, Italy was also subject to an embargo on the export of arms and military vehicles, but some vehicles remained in service in countries that had purchased the AS 42 and its variants. Spain, in particular, continued to use Italian vehicles for several years, while some other countries fell back on domestically produced armored vehicles or those of different origins.

Exports of vehicles such as the AS 42 were a minor part of Italy's wartime economy, but they helped solidify ties between Fascist Italy and allied and neutral nations during the conflict, as well as providing technical support for rebuilding the armed forces of some postwar countries.

▲ From top left: a Lince armoured car on parade in Padua with the police force in 1950. Right: an AS 42 Saharaian armoured car full of partisans celebrating the end of the war. Large photo: a *Beute Panzerspähwagen Lince 202(i)* of the 13th Panzer-Division on the streets of Bologna, with three captured Gurkha soldiers sitting on top of the engine compartment.

BIBLIOGRAPHY

- Nicola Pignato, *Storia dei mezzi corazzati*, Fratelli Fabbri editori, 1976, pp. 81-88.
- Enrico Finazzer, Luigi Carretta *Le Camionette del Regio Esercito*. Gruppo Modellistico Trentino di studio e ricerca storica
- Paolo Crippa. *I reparti corazzati della Repubblica Sociale Italiana 1943/1945*. Marvia edizioni
- Bruno Benvenuti e Ugo F. Colonna - *L'armamento italiano nella seconda guerra mondiale Carri armati in servizio fra le due guerre 1* - Edizioni Bizzarri, Roma 1972
- Filippo Cappellano, *Gli autoveicoli da combattimento dell'Esercito Italiano, vol.1 e 2*, Ufficio Storico dello Stato Maggiore dell'Esercito, Roma 2002.
- Jentz LT, Regenberg W., *Panzer tracts No. 19-2 Beute Panzerkampfwagen, carri armati britannici, americani, russi e italiani catturati dal 1940 al 1945*, Panzer Tracts, 2008
- N. Pignato, "*I mezzi blindo-corazzati italiani 1923-1943*", Albertelli Edizioni Speciali, Parma, 2004.
- Giulio Benussi, *Semicingolati, Motoveicoli e Veicoli Speciali del Regio Esercito Italiano 1919-1943* – Edizioni Intergest – 1976
- John Joseph Timothy Sweet, Iron Arm: *The Mechanization of Mussolini's Army, 1920-1940*, Stackpole Books, 2007
- Emiliano Ciaralli *Le Forze Armate, 1935* – Colonel Pederzini, Italian Tanks 1917-1945.
- Nico Sgarlato *Corazzati Italiani 1939-1945*, War Set n°10, 2006.
- David Vannucci, *Corazzati e blindati italiani dalle origini allo scoppio della seconda guerra mondiale*, Editrice Innocenti, 2003.
- Daniele Guglielmi & David Zambon, *Les véhicules blindés italiens 1910/43 (1ère partie)*, Batailles & Blindés n°24, 2008.
- Lucio Ceva & Andrea Curami, *La meccanizzazione dell'esercito dalle origini al 1943, Tomo II*, USSME, 1994
- Ugo Barlozzetti & Alberto Pirella *Mezzi dell'Esercito Italiano 1935-45*, Editoriale Olimpia, 1986
- Ralph Riccio, Marcello Calzolari e Nicola Pignato, *Italian Tanks and Combat Vehicles of World War II*, Roadrunner Mattioli, 2010
- Alberto Pirella, *Autoblindo dell'asse: autoblindo italo-tedesche 1920 - 1945*, Ciarrapico 1977
- Paolo Crippa e Carlo Cucut *I reparti corazzati italiani nei Balcani*, Soldiershop 2019.
- Paolo Crippa. *I reparti corazzati del R.E. E l'armistizio 1° Volume*, Soldiershop 2021.
- Paolo Crippa. *I reparti corazzati del R.E. E l'armistizio 2° Volume*, Soldiershop 2021.
- Crippa P. e Manes L., *Carri Armati "Partigiani"*, Witness to War, Volume 34, aprile 2022
- Arturo Giusti, *Le camionette della Repubblica Sociale Italiana 1943-45*, Soldiershop 2024
- Mario Pieri / Guglielmi Daniele / Riccio Ralph - *Automezzi Italiani DellaSeconda Guerra Mondiale*, Gruppo Modellistico trentino 2023.
- T.Vendrame, A.Bondesan *Ruote nel deserto. Teatri operativi, mobilità e logistica del Regio Esercito in Africa Settentrionale*, Cierre edizioni 2022

PUBLISHED TITLES

TWE-035 EN

www.ingramcontent.com/pod-product-compliance
Lightning Source LLC
LaVergne TN
LVHW072120060526
838201LV00068B/4931